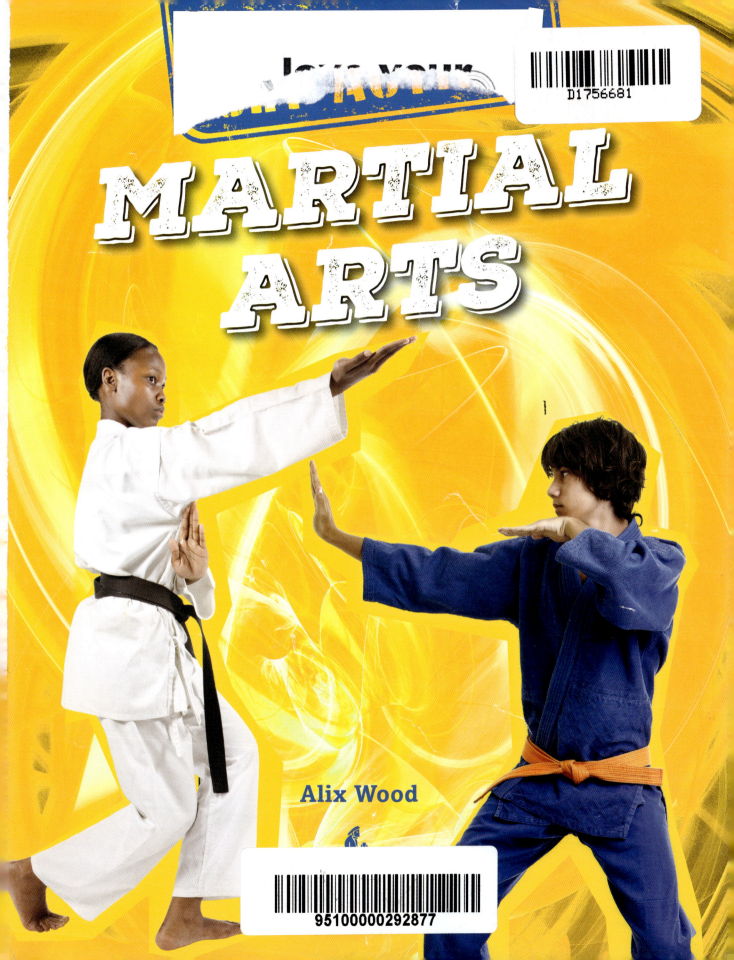

Love your

MARTIAL ARTS

Alix Wood

Wayland
First Published in Great Britain in 2019 by Wayland.

Produced for Wayland by Alix Wood
Art direction and content research: Kevin Wood
Editor: Eloise Macgregor
Editor for Gareth Stevens: Kerri O'Donnell
Consultant: James Latus, Kernow Martial Arts

HB ISBN: 978 1 5263 1170 2
PB ISBN: 978 1 5263 1171 9

Photo credits:
Cover, 1, 4, 6, 10, 14, 22 top, 30 © Shutterstock; 18 © Photostock10/Shutterstock; 26 © Rob Wilson/Shutterstock; 3 © istock; 19 © Chris Robbins; all other images © Greg Dennis.

Acknowledgments
With grateful thanks to Finnian Cooling, Josh Latus, Storm Brennon, Kieron Turk, Will Ferris, Corie Stubbs and Ellena Harrison.

Printed in China

Wayland
An imprint of
Hachette Children's Group
Part of Hodder & Stoughton
Carmelite House
50 Victoria Embankment
London EC4Y 0DZ

An Hachette UK Comany
www.hachette.co.uk
www.hachettechildrens.co.uk

MIX
Paper from
responsible sources
FSC® C104740
FSC
www.fsc.org

CONTENTS

WHY DO MARTIAL ARTS?

Martial arts can be fun to learn. They can improve your health and fitness, too. It is interesting to learn about the heritage, language and tradition of the different martial arts.

There is a style of martial arts to suit everyone. Tae kwon do is very different from the gentler aikido or kung fu. Some styles are great for combat or self-defence. Other styles focus more on **meditation** and building on your inner strength.

In aikido students learn to focus on **harmony** as well as self-defence.

Judo involves a lot of floor work, grappling and trying to put your opponent off-balance.

It is important to warm up before a martial arts session. Warming up stops you from pulling muscles. Gently stretch all the major muscles. If you feel any pain, stop and try a different stretch.

1. To do a shoulder stretch (left), stand with your shoulders relaxed. Reach one arm across your chest, **parallel** to the floor. Place your other hand on the elbow. Gently pull your elbow in toward your chest. Hold the stretch. Repeat with the other arm.

2. Press-ups (below) work the chest, arms and shoulders.

TRY THIS

Try this standing leg stretch to warm up your hamstrings. Stand with your legs wider than shoulder width. Keep your back straight and then reach down between your feet.

You could try to gently lean towards each foot to stretch even more.

AIKIDO

Aikido is a Japanese martial art and a form of self-defence. It uses locks, holds, throws and your opponent's own movements to combat any form of attack.

Aikido moves are done by **blending** with the motion of your opponent. You redirect the force of the attack rather than hitting it head-on. In aikido, mental training is as important as physical training. Aikido teaches the student to face conflict and not run away from it, but it does not **advocate** violence.

In aikido, some people wear wide pleated dark trousers called hakama. It is a tradition that the highest ranking student has to fold the teacher's hakama (below) as a token of respect. It's not easy!

The word 'aikido' means 'the way of harmony of the spirit'. 'Ai' means 'harmony,' 'ki' means 'spirit' and 'do' means 'way'. Ki is the life energy thought to be in all things. People who practice aikido will meditate to help them concentrate on their inner energy, breathing and heart rate.

Different martial arts have different ways of standing, called stances. A correct stance helps keep you balanced, ready to attack or defend. Aikido has the simplest stances to learn, as it only has one main stance!

harmony

spirit

way

TRY THIS

The main stance in aikido is called hanmi. You need to keep your back straight and your head up. In left hanmi the toes of your right foot turn slightly outwards. The middle of your right foot should be lined up behind your left heel. Your left shoulder is over your left hip and your right shoulder is over your right hip. For right hanmi, do the same but with opposite feet and shoulder position.

Irime and Tenkan

One of the most important aspects of aikido is to keep yourself safe by moving out of the way of an attack. The two main methods are called irime and tenkan.

Both methods make you take a step towards your opponent, **pivot** and end up safe by their side. You use the force of your opponent to your advantage, by helping them continue in the direction they were moving, and moving yourself out of harm's way!

Irime

Stand in hanmi. As your opponent goes to punch you, get ready to grab their arm.

Slide your front foot forwards. The slide makes your body turn and the punch will miss. Grab your opponent's arm as shown.

Keeping your feet in the same position. Pivot around to face the other way. Pull your opponent's arm using the force from their punch.

Your body position and the opponent's own force will make them lose their balance and fall.

Tenkan

'Tenkan' means 'turning'. Stand with your left foot forward if your attacker is using their right hand. Grab your opponent's right wrist with your left hand.

Keep your front foot in position. Lift your back foot and step around to face the other way. Now you are standing beside your opponent. Pull on their wrist to get them to lose their balance.

KUNG FU

Kung fu is a Chinese martial art. There are many different styles of kung fu. All styles use throws, holds, weapons and self-defence. Some styles mimic the movements of animals.

The ancient Chinese symbol of yin and yang (right) is often used as a symbol of tai chi, a form of kung fu. Its design shows two opposite forces working together. In kung fu, strength and gentleness are the opposite forces.

Tradition and respect are very important in martial arts. Kung fu practitioners show respect to their opponents and their teacher by doing a special salute.

To do a kung fu standing salute put your right open hand over your left clenched fist. Wrap your hand around the fist and bow from the waist. Look the person you are saluting in the eye as you bow.

TRY THIS

Try these kung fu kicks

Spin Back Kick
Face your opponent and lift up one knee.
Spin round on the other foot by pushing your hip
round and then aim the kick behind you. Aim at
or below the waist with this back kick.

Side kick
Raise one knee
and strike out
to the side.
Strike with the
outer edge of
your foot.

Low kick
Snap your lower leg out from
the knee and aim the sole and
heel of your foot at a low target.

Front Snap Kick

To perform a good kung fu front snap kick, remember the snap! It is important that the leg kicks out and returns back quickly.

You start the kick with your foot **flexed** and your toe pointing down. When your leg kicks out you snap your foot up quickly, so that the top of your foot hits the target.

Step forwards and lift the knee of your kicking leg.
Swing out from your knee, not your hip.

4

5

Don't snap your leg out too hard at first, as you could damage your knee.

Bring your lower leg back fast. Your opponent could grab it otherwise.

TRY THIS

Try this kung fu heel kick

With your toes back, thrust your heel at the target. At the same time, bring your arms back powerfully, with your fists clenched. This adds power to your kick. Try to straighten your non-kicking leg at the same time.

JUJITSU

Jujitsu is a martial art from Japan. It was developed as a way of defeating an armoured armed opponent using no weapon. Jujitsu means 'the gentle art'.

Jujitsu relies on **technique** rather than strength. Like aikido, jujitsu uses the force of an attacker and turns it against him. Strikes in jujitsu are usually distractions to weaken an opponent so that a hold or lock can be applied. A hammerfist is a strike with the bottom of a clenched fist. It is often used to strike an opponent's wrist when blocking punches.

A hammerfist strike

Jujitsu is the martial art used by medieval warriors of Japan called the **samurai**. The samurai came from noble families, and were fierce fighters.

When you learn jujitsu you will learn how to block an attack, and then how to apply locks and holds. The purpose of blocking techniques is to stop the opponent's punch, kick, strike or grab from succeeding. There are several different types of block.

TRY THIS

Try doing this low outward block

Pair up with a friend and ask them to direct a low kick toward you. Obviously, don't actually kick each other! Outwards blocks move the blow to the side. Inward blocks move the blow across your body. For this outward block, turn sideways so your body becomes a narrower target. Sweep the leg away to the left with your arm.

Blocks

You can do blocks with either arm, depending on how you are standing and where your opponent throws the punch.

Forearm block

The forearm block is used when your attacker throws a straight punch. At the same time as you block the strike, bring your **opposite** hand down powerfully to your hip. This means you are ready with that hand to react to any future moves.

Blocks 1, 2 and 3 are all basic forearm blocks. Blocks 1 and 2 both use the same arm. Block 1 sweeps the arm to the right and block 2 sweeps it away to the left.

Block number 3 uses the opposite arm to sweep to the left. You can also use the opposite arm to sweep to the right.

A high block is used against blows aimed at the head.

High block
Stand in the ready position, with your hands up to guard your head. Place one foot slightly in front of the other, so you are balanced if you lean backwards or forwards.

As the punch is thrown, raise your left arm with elbow bent and fist rotated upwards. This fist acts as a hook to sweep the punch away. Meet the punch with your forearm and move your arm up and left.

JUDO

Judo is a martial art that started in Japan. Judo uses balance, quick movements and **leverage** to beat an opponent. A small person can beat a much larger one once they have mastered these skills.

Judo developed from jujitsu and is similar in many ways. Judo mainly involves throws, locks and holds. It is important to keep your balance and to unbalance your opponent.

unbalancing an opponent in a judo competition

In judo you need a good grip to hold on to your opponent. With a good grip you can control your opponent, and throw him or her to the ground. The basic judo grip is the sleeve-lapel grip.

To do a sleeve-lapel grip, hold your opponent's right sleeve with your left hand. Hold their left lapel with your right hand. Your opponent will grip you in the same manner.

There are several other grips you can use. You can grip both sleeves or both lapels. In competitions you can be penalised if you do not move from either of these grips for six or more seconds without mounting an attack.

TRY THIS

Stand in a low crouch with legs wide apart, knees bent outwards, and body leaning slightly forwards. This defensive position makes it difficult for an opponent to throw you.

Breaking Balance

Balance, and breaking your opponent's balance, is an important skill of judo. You need to learn about the centre of gravity.

The centre of gravity is the centre of an object's weight. As you start to wobble forwards, your centre of gravity goes forwards, and you are off-balance. You can get your opponent off-balance by pushing or pulling the opposite way you actually want your opponent to go. As you push, your opponent will resist by leaning his or her full weight towards you. Then it is easy to pull them down, using their force as well as your own. Leg reaps also disrupt your opponent's balance.

Grip your opponent and lift your right leg.

Pull your opponent towards you. Hook your right leg around their right leg.

Now push your opponent backwards and they will fall.

Try to keep hold of them as they fall so you can hold them down.

TRY THIS

Here's how to counter a leg reap if someone tries to do one on you. Quickly step back before your opponent has managed to hook around your leg. Lean forwards and lift your back leg, with their leg still resting on it. This will put them off-balance. You will then be able to throw them.

KARATE

Karate is a Japanese martial art. The word 'karate' means 'empty hand', meaning it uses no weapons. Karate experts harden their hands so they can perform breaking exercises. Don't try breaking bricks without putting in years of practice first!

Karate uses kicks, strikes, chops and punches as its weapons. A punch is a strike made with the fist. It is important to make a tight fist so you don't hurt your hand.

1. Fold your fingertips in tightly towards your hands.

2. Then fold into a fist.

3. Wrap your thumb around the fist. Never put the thumb under your fingers.

To practise your punches you can start from either ready position in picture 1 or 2. Make sure your fists are correctly made, with your thumb over your fingers.

Pull your right hand back so it is upside down by your right side.

Twist your arms when you punch. The punching arm twists to turn the fist so it points down. At the same time the other arm twists so the fist faces up.

Punch forwards with your right hand while, at the same time pulling the left hand back.

Punches and Chops

There is a saying in karate circles that there is no first strike in karate. A good karate practitioner should never start any attack. However, in self-defence, karate strikes are very effective.

When you make a strike in karate, it is important to focus on speed and power. The reverse punch is a very effective strike. Step forward onto your left foot at the same time as you punch with your right fist. Rotate from your waist and hips. The punch's power then comes from your fist, wrist, elbow and hips all at once.

TRY THIS

Try shouting 'Ee-ya!' when you make a strike. It helps you release energy at the right time.

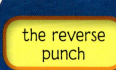

the reverse punch

Karate chop

Raise your right hand behind your ear and hold left hand slightly forwards.

Snap your arm and strike while pulling your left arm tight to your waist.

Bring your right hand around.

TRY THIS

A karate chop is a strike with the side of the hand. It is also sometimes called a knife hand. Strike with the bottom edge of your hand, between the knuckle of your little finger and your wrist. Don't hit with your fingers, as it will hurt.

TAE KWON DO

Tae kwon do is a Korean martial art. It is well known for its kicking techniques. It was thought that the hands were too valuable to be used in combat, so the feet were favoured. However, hands are still used for some techniques.

In tae kwon do, points are given for kicks to the body protector and the head. Points are deducted for fouls. Adult competitors are paired by their weight.

TRY THIS

Learn your kicking distance so you do not miss. Get a training pad and a friend and take turns holding the pad while the other takes a kick.

Tae kwon do competitors usually wear protective gear when they spar.

Fancy kicks are great, but if your attacker is at close range you'll need to use your hands. Tae kwon do teaches some strike techniques too.

Backfist strike

Stand in a fighting stance, sideways to your opponent. Hold both hands up with your shoulders down.

Move one forearm across your body, and your striking forearm above it and across your shoulder.

Pivot your striking arm up and, at the same time, draw your other hand in to your waist. The target area is the bridge of the nose.

Kicks

Tae kwon do is well known for its kicking techniques. The leg is the longest and strongest weapon a martial artist has, so kicks give you the best chance of landing a powerful strike without being hit back.

Axe Kick

Start in a fighting stance.

Shift your weight forwards.

Kick your leg up and then strike with your heel.

Roundhouse kick

1 From a fighting stance, bring your right leg up.

2 Keep your foot as far behind as possible.

3 Push your leg out and around. Fully extend your leg and strike with the ball of the foot.

GLOSSARY

advocate To speak in favour of or argue for something

blending Shading or merging into each other

centre of gravity The point at which the entire weight of a body is concentrated

flexed To move your muscles so your foot is at an angle

harmony Living in agreement with others

leverage The action of a lever or the increase in force gained by using a lever

meditation Time spent in quiet thinking

opposite An object at the other end, side or corner, for example your left hand is the opposite hand to your right hand

parallel Lying or moving in the same direction but always the same distance apart

pivot To turn on the spot

samurai Warriors serving a Japanese feudal lord and practising a code of conduct which valued honour over life

technique The basic physical movements that are used

FOR MORE INFORMATION

Books

Nixon, James, *First Sport: Martial Arts.* Franklin Watts, 2017.

Page, Jason, *Martial Arts, Boxing, and Other Combat Sports: Fencing, Judo, Wrestling, Taekwondo, & A Whole Lot More (Olympic Sports)*, Crabtree Publishing, 2008.

Websites

BBC Get Inspired: How to get into Martial Arts
www.bbc.co.uk/sport/get-inspired/23436235
Gives information and advice about getting into martial arts.

World Martial Arts Information Centre
www.martialinfo.com
A guide to the world of martial arts.

INDEX